MOTHER EARTH'S

A Quilted Alphabet & Story Book

INSPIRED BY *Mother Earth and Her Children*
BY SIBYLLE VON OLFERS

Sieglinde Schoen Smith

Breckling Press

Library of Congress Cataloging-in-Publication Data
Schoen Smith, Sieglinde,
Mother Earth's ABC : a quilted alphabet and story book / Sieglinde Schoen Smith.
p. cm.
"Inspired by Mother Earth and her children by Sibylle von Olfers."
ISBN 978-1-933308-20-3
1. Quilting. 2. Appliqué. 3. Alphabet in art. I. Title.

TT835.S34843 2008
746.46'043-dc22

2008002004

This book was set in Carlton Regular
Poem by Anne Knudsen
Editorial and art direction by Anne Knudsen
Interior and cover design by Maria Mann
Photography by Cathy Meals

Published by Breckling Press
283 N. Michigan St, Elmhurst, IL 60126

Printed and bound in China
International Standard Book Number (ISBN 13): 978-1-933308-20-3

A seedling sleeps

Beneath frozen trees,

Eyes peep open. Limbs reach
out in mighty yawns.

Fairy child awakening
         finds that she has...

Grown.

Huddled in her tight-wrapped bud,
she breaks through frosted ground.

I am here, she smiles.

Joy, oh joy, to feel
the sun's sweet rays.

eeping her cloak of green
curled about her,

Lightly she steps into the

orning dew. A golden
world is waiting.

Nimbly she dances. Her arms

Outstretch to reveal flashes
of red and fiery orange within.

Perfect blossoms gently open
to the skies. Too soon the

Quiet beauty of Spring
makes way for the

Riotous pleasures of...

Summer.

Tumbling in the heady breeze,
her brilliant petals

Umbrella down to earth with
tiny dust specks on their backs.

iolets, reds, or yellow golds?
She imagines the

Wondrous colors her seeds
    will bring to the earth.

Xtraordinary.

Yesterday's sleeping seedling
is next year's newborn...

Zinnia.

The illustrated letters in this book are inspired by a quilt made by Sieglinde Schoen Smith. Named *Mother Earth and Her Children*, the quilt retells an old German folk tale, in which children make the world ready for Spring. It's easy to use these beautiful letters in your own sewing project. You can make your own pillow, placemat, or a quilt with your name on it.

You may use any method of appliqué you please to make the letters. Sieglinde uses traditional needleturn appliqué, which she learned as a child in Germany. Begin by tracing each part of each letter and transferring the image to fabric. Sieglinde uses batik fabrics in pretty Spring shades, made by Hoffman California Fabrics. She cuts each letter part out, leaving about 1/8" extra fabric all around. She turns the extra fabric under and presses. Next, she pins the letter pieces in place onto her background fabric. With little stitches and matching thread, Sieglinde sews all around each piece. (The pages at the back of the book show the sewing sequence for each piece of each letter.) Look closely and you'll see that every appliqué piece is then outlined by a row of black embroidery stitches, called stem stitch. If you prefer, you can sew down your pieces using a sewing machine, then outline them with stem stitch or machine embroidery.

Even faster, try photocopying the designs onto fabric sheets. To make this easy, check out *Mother Earth's ABC: Photo Transfer Pack and CD*, described on the next-to-last page of the book. You can then cut the letters out and sew them by hand or machine. Faster still, you can use a product called fusible web to iron the letters onto a background fabric. Fusible web makes the back of each letter sticky, so that when you iron over it, the letter sticks or fuses onto the background.

Embroidery makes the pretty details on flowers, butterflies, and woodland creatures sing! Sieglinde uses just three basic stitches. Perfect embroidery takes dedication and practice. If you are not experienced, ask for help.

Sieglinde learned a technique she calls *layered embroidery* (LE) in Germany and she uses it to create texture and subtle shading on her children's faces, butterfly wings, and more. Use single-strand DMC embroidery floss and a stitch length of no more than 3/8". (You will need to go much narrower for flower stems.) The rows are shown in different colors here for clarity, but you can use the same or varied colors for different effects. Repeat rows 1, 2, and 3 as necessary to fill each area of the design.

Row 1

Row 2

Row 3

Each appliqué letter is outlined in black using a form of back stitch or *stem stitch* (SS). It is also used for drawing details like butterfly antennae. Come up at A, make a slant stitch to B, then come up again at C, half way along the previous stitch. Continue along the entire design.

C
A B

Details like eyes or spots are done with *French knots* (FK). Bring the needle up through the fabric at an angle, then twist the thread around it two or three times. Push the needle back through the fabric, very close to the entry point.

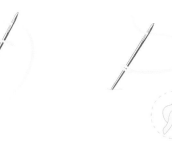

The pages that follow show the correct sequence in which to appliqué each part of each letter. They also help you see which parts of each image are embroidered. LE stands for layered embroidery; FK stands for French knot. SS stands for stem stitch

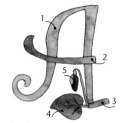

Appliqué sequence: 1, 2, 3, 4, 5
Embroidery: LE for stems, bud cap; SS for outlines/details

Embroidery: LE and FK for butterfly; SS for outlines/details

Appliqué sequence: 1, 2, 3
Embroidery: LE for bumblebee body; SS for outlines/details

Appliqué sequence: 1 through 6
Embroidery: LE for stamens, stems, bud caps; SS for outlines/details

Appliqué sequence: 1, 2, 3
Embroidery: LE for stems, flowers, bud caps; SS for outlines/details

Appliqué sequence: 1 through 6
Embroidery: LE for stems, leaves, flower center, buds; SS for outlines/details

Appliqué sequence: 1, 2
Embroidery: LE for spider; SS for web, outlines/details

Embroidery: LE for stems, leaves, flowers; SS for outlines/details

Appliqué sequence: 1, 2, 3
Embroidery: LE for bird body, eye, beak, leaves; SS for outlines/details

Appliqué sequence: 1 through 16
Embroidery: FK for buds; SS for outlines/details

Embroidery: LE for stems, flowers; SS for outlines

Appliqué sequence: 1 through 8
Embroidery: LE for stems, leaves, buds; SS for outlines/details

Appliqué sequence: 1, 2
Embroidery: LE for mouse, squirrel, nut; SS for outlines/details

Embroidery: LE for butterfly; SS for outlines/details

Embroidery: LE for deer; SS for outlines/details

Appliqué sequence: 1 through 5
Embroidery: LE for flower center, stems, leaves, bud caps; SS outlines/details

Appliqué sequence: 1 through 5
Embroidery: LE for grass stalks, white spots; SS for outlines/details

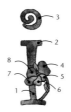

Appliqué sequence: 1 through 8
Embroidery: LE for stem, leaf, flower center; SS for outlines/details

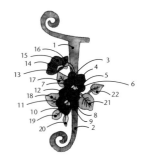

Appliqué sequence: 1 through 22
Embroidery: LE for stems, flower centers; SS for outlines/details

Appliqué sequence: 1 through 7
Embroidery: LE for stem and leaf; SS for outlines/details

Appliqué sequence: 1 through 15
Embroidery: LE for stems, leaves, buds; SS for outlines/details

Appliqué sequence: 1, 2
Embroidery: LE for bumblebee; SS for outlines/details

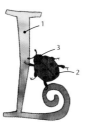

Appliqué sequence: 1, 2, 3
Embroidery: LE for black spots, legs; SS for outlines/details

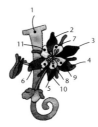

Appliqué sequence: 1 through 11
Embroidery: LE for buds, stamens, stems, leaf; SS for outlines/details

Appliqué sequence: 1, 2
Embroidery: LE for flowers, stems, small leaves, butterfly; SS for outlines/details

Embroidery: LE for birds; SS for outlines/details

Embroidery: LE for leaves; ; SS for outlines/details

Embroidery: LE for grasshopper; SS for outlines/details

Appliqué sequence: 1 through 5
Embroidery: LE for eyes, beak, feet; SS for outlines/details

Embroidery: LE for snail; SS for outlines/details

Embroidery: LE for fox; SS for outlines/details

Embroidery: LE for frog, trumpet; SS for outlines/details

Appliqué sequence: 1 through 6
Embroidery: LE for butterfly body; SS for outlines/details

Appliqué sequence: 1 through 9
Embroidery: LE for stems, bud caps; SS for outlines/details

Embroider: LE for bird; SS for outlines/details

Embroidery: LE for mouse; SS for outlines/details

Embroidery: LE for robin; SS for outlines/details

Embroidery: LE for bumblebee; SS for outlines/details

Appliqué sequence: 1 through 15
Embroidery: LE for stems; flower center, SS for outlines/details

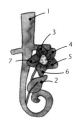

Appliqué sequence: 1 through 7
Embroidery: LE for flower center, stems; FK for dots; SS for outlines/details

Appliqué sequence: 1, 2, 3, 4
Embroidery: LE for dragonfly, frog eyes, black spots; SS for outlines/details

Embroidery: LE for bumblebee; SS for outlines/details

Appliqué sequence: 1 through 11
Embroidery: LE for flower center; FK for yeollow dots; SS for outlines/details

Embroidery: LE flower, stems, leaves. SS for outlines/details

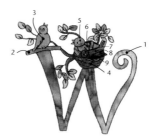

Appliqué sequence: 1 through 9
Embroidery: LE for bird beaks, eyes, feet, leaves, stems; SS for outlines/details

Appliqué sequence: 1, 2
Embroidery: LE bug head, spots, flower; SS for black outlines/details

Appliqué sequence: 1 through 5
Embroidery: LE beetle legs, candle, holder; SS for outlines/details

Embroidery: LE flowers and leaves; SS for grass, stems, outlines/details

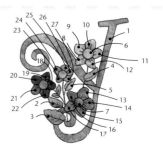

Appliqué sequence: 1 through 27
Embroidery: LE for leaves of leftmost flower; SS for stems, outlines/details

Appliqué sequence: 1 through 5
Embroidery: LE for flowers; SS for stems, outlines/details

Appliqué sequence: 1 through 4
Embroidery: LE for face, hair; SS for outlines/details

Appliqué sequence: 1, 2, 3, 4
Embroidery: LE for flower; SS for stem, outlines/details

Also by Sieglinde Schoen Smith

Mother Earth's ABC: Photo-Transfer Pack and CD

Achieve the beautiful effects of Sieglinde's needleturn appliqué and embroidery on your computer! This image-transfer pack includes a CD with hi-res images of every letter in *Mother Earth and Her Children*. Using any computer design program, you can import these .tif files, then resize them to suit your project. When you are ready, print your color letters out onto photo-transfers sheets. Now you are ready to sew or fuse the images onto your sewing projects! The Photo-Transfer Pack includes: CD with high-resolution of 52 upper case and lower case letters (PC and Mac compatible); Set of five photo-transfer fabric sheets, 8-½" x 11".
UPC. 8-82383-00029-3

Mother Earth and Her Children: Jigsaw Puzzle and Poster

Recreate the images in Sieglinde's award-winning quilt, one piece at a time. Puzzle enthusiasts will enjoy the intricate detail in the illustrations. As an added bonus, quilters will love the oversize poster of Sieglinde's quilt.
750 piece jigsaw puzzle, measuring 22" x 14". Color poster, measuring 30" x 18".
UPC: 8-82383-00031-6

Mother Earth's Quilt Sampler: Five Appliqué Patterns Inspired by *Mother Earth and Her Children*

Make your own quilt inspired by *Mother Earth and Her Children*! This beautiful sampler book includes patterns for five quilts using the same images found in Sieglinde's popular children's book. There is a quilt for each season, Spring, Summer, Fall, and Winter, plus a bonus project, titled The Quilting Bee. Each finished quilt measures about 36" x 48". The book includes complete instructions and pull-out templates sheets.
128 pages, deluxe paperback with flaps.
ISBN: 978-1933308-22-7 UPC: 8-82383-00030-9

For more information contact Breckling Press at 800-951-7826 (630-941-1179 outside US)
or visit www.brecklingpress.com

SIBYLLE VON OLFERS
MOTHER EARTH
AND HER CHILDREN
A Quilted Fairy Tale

ILLUSTRATIONS SIEGLINDE SCHOEN SMITH TRANSLATION JACK ZIPES

Mother Earth and Her Children: A Quilted Fairy Tale

Spring approaches and Mother Earth wakes her sleepy children. Soon all hands are busy, stitching new clothes in bright Spring colors. The children dust off the bumblebees and paint spendid new coats on the ladybugs. When everyone is ready, they lead a colorful procession up through the earth, where the children become the flowers of Summer. This delightful new translation of Sibylle von Olfers' classic German tale is illustrated with Sieglinde's award-winning quilt.

32 pages, hardcover with jacket.

ISBN: 978-1933308-18-0, UPC: 8-82383-0027-9